IMAGES OF ENGLAND

Chalford
to Sapperton

George Juggins, 1960s, having just collected his winter fuel from Coal Merchants J.H. Smart & Son.

Previous page: This is believed to be the Holmes family, 1880s. The boys later became Chalford businessmen.

IMAGES OF ENGLAND

Chalford
to Sapperton

Stanley Gardiner

NONSUCH

A well-known Chalford view down the valley from Coppice Hill, c. 1902.

Opposite: George and Arthur Mills with dog Spot at Ashmeads Mill, an enlargement from the print on page 41.

Front cover illustration: The Cane and Binding Shop of the Chalford Stick Co. at St Mary's Mill, c. 1905.

First published 1995
This new pocket edition 2006
Images unchanged from first edition

Nonsuch Publishing Limited
The Mill, Brimscombe Port,
Stroud, Gloucestershire, GL5 2QG
www.nonsuch-publishing.com

Nonsuch Publishing is an imprint of Tempus Publishing Group

British Library Cataloguing in Publication Data.
A catalogue record for this book is available from the British Library.

ISBN 1-84588-259-8

Typesetting and origination by Nonsuch Publishing Limited
Printed in Great Britain by Oaklands Book Services Limited

Contents

Acknowledgements

The preparation of this book has been rendered easier by the willing help of friends, acquaintances, and the staff of the Chalford Publishing Company Ltd.

I am indebted to Mrs Penrose for the loan of two wonderful views of St. Mary's Mill by H.J. Comley, the Stroud photographer. Also to my late colleague, Lionel Padin, without whose ability to find, and borrow, old photographs, family albums and documents, such a selection as is shown here could not have been prepared.

Again I am indebted to colleagues and acquaintances: Reg Clarke, Eddie Cuss, John Denley, Bob Gardiner, Alec Jones, Mike Mills, Bob Pearman, Pat Pinnell, Iris Swainger, for the background information so necessary for interpreting these old photographs.

Finally, my grateful thanks to all those who, through the last twenty-five years, have loaned all the material for copying, willingly allowing its use in slide shows and books. So many of their names were locked in Lionel's memory, but I trust that this word of thanks will show my appreciation.

I must not forget my grateful thanks to my wife, Nancy, for tolerating the clutter of prints, albums, books, etc. that were scattered around for several weeks during the preparation of this book.

Introduction

This book is intended to show village scenes and life of bygone times in an area which, roughly, covers the four miles of the Golden Valley from from St Mary's, at Chalford West to Sapperton, and includes the villages one mile either side. Therefore its range covers a semi-industrialised area and Cotswold villages, those villages being, to a great extent, the product of the industrial vale, which is itself the product of the power of the River Frome.

Chalford Vale Village seems to have had its centres at points where the old upland trackways crossed the River Frome, those centres expanding as water-powered industries developed. Migrants first built their homes on the steep northern sides of the valley giving rise to Chalford's alpine character, then gradually occupied sites on the upper slopes, eventually spilling over on to the upland plateau of Nash End Common. By that practice they were always in danger of being amerced at the Manor Court for purloining pieces of the Lord's land. In the late Middle Ages many migrants came from the Low Countries bringing their weaving skills with them. Many settled in the area, leaving evidence in names of places and family names, for instance France Lynch; Webb; Weaver; Clutterbuck; Corderoy.

The Far Oakridge of today used to be Oakridge – the ridge of the oaks – on the edge of the plateau of Oakridge Common, while the Oakridge of today was Oakridge Lynch, very akin in style to Chalford and France Lynches. Both are sufficiently close to Chalford to have shared in the woollen and silk industries, besides having an agricultural background. Oakridge Lynch even had a silk mill of its own.

Sapperton retained its agricultural basis, centred on Cirencester, as its market town. It was a Domesday village, and had two mills. Daneway came into prominence with the building of the Thames & Severn Canal, especially the tunnel through the Cotswold scarp. Frampton Mansell, too, has its manorial origins, and also possessed woollen mills at Puck's and Bakers (or Twissels) Mill.

The villages have had their share of nationally-renouned figures. Roger Bacon, the thirteenth-century scholar, was born at Toadsmoor (near Circencester, not Ilchester as erroneously transcribed). He received his early education, legend says, at a cell at St Mary's House, but most probably at the medieval chapel at Brownshill, on the hill above St Mary's. Then, the eighteenth-century Astronomer Royal James Bradley, responsible for the reform of the calendar in 1752, married Mary Peach of St Mary's House, and lived and died there. His successor as Astronomer Royal, Nathaniel Bliss, son of the clothier at Bliss Mills, was born at St Mary's House. At the Valley Inn, Chalford East, John Thomas was born. As a teenager he was apprenticed to a sculptor, becoming so proficient that he came to the notice of Sir Charles Barry of Birmingham. When the Houses of Parliament were destroyed by fire in 1836 Barry was commissioned to rebuild them. He put Thomas in charge of the stonemasons and carvers in the rebuilding.

Gloucestershire's great seventeenth-century historian, Sir Robert Atkyns, lived at Sapperton, both at Sapperton House and Pinbury Park. Two hundred years later, Ernest Gimson and Ernest and Sidney Barnsley moved their craft workshops from London to Pinbury Park. Ten years later they moved to Sapperton, building their houses there and·having their workshops at Daneway House. On Gimson's death in 1919, those workshops were moved to Hallidays Mill at Chalford under the direction of his foreman, Peter Waals.

Oakridge too has its famous people – Sir William Rothenstein, artist; William Simmonds, sculptor; John Drinkwater, dramatist; Max Beerbohm, caricaturist; Sir Stafford Cripps, Chancellor of the Exchequer; and Sir Brian Robertson, Chairman of British Rail; to name but a few.

The whole area, therefore, was steeped in history which the intrepid Victorian and Edwardian photographers could use. Besides national photographers the Stroud area had many local photographers, professionals and gifted amateurs, who, perhaps, are best described as 'snap-happy'. They have left us a wonderful legacy. For the Chalford area, the most famous was Frank Colville, and as many of his photographs as can be positively attributed to him are included.

Many of the pictures herein have not been printed in book form before, but enough have been found to provide a sequential tour of the area. They have been chosen not only to show how the area has altered during this century, but also to illustrate how lifestyle and dress have changed, and how 'making one's own entertainment' used to be the norm. The choice has also been based on audience reaction when these prints have been shown as slides at the numerous slide shows given by myself and my colleagues over the last twenty-two years. Captions endeavour to follow these reactions.

Therefore I hope that, in perusing this book, you, reader, can sit, relax, and indulge in a slower tempo of life.

One

Chalford Vale

St Mary's Mill, c. 1905. The Chalford Stick Co. was founded by W.C. Dann in 1902 and continued here for some seventy years. Previously the mill had been a woollen mill and a flock mill.

The male workforce, *c.* 1908-10. W.C. Dann, wearing a trilby hat, is in the back row on the left.

The female workforce, *c.* 1908-10. W.C. Dann is on the left.

The original was a multi-coloured poster for exports to the Far East. The languages depicted have been identified as Chinese, Bengali, Gujerati, and Burmese.

Thames & Severn Canal above St Mary's Lock, *c.* 1912. The building on the left is Clayfields Mill, abutting the main road (A419). The small building in front was once a mill. It was to be the first Meeting Room for Chalford W.I., but collapsed before use.

The Wheelwrights – Bennetts, 1920/2. George, Bert, and Bill, with a near neighbour, Chris Grange, a railcar driver. The workshop was in the part of Clayfields Mill abutting the main road.

A view from 1873 showing Clayfields Mill (left) and Victoria Silk Mill (right). Front centre is the pine end of Iles Mill which, having no chimney, would have then been water-powered.

Compare this similar view dating from 1898. Behind the tall Vale House there is now a terrace at right angles across the road, and a row of houses in front of the Silk Mill beyond the canal.

That row of houses opposite the Silk Mill, c. 1912. The mill had been converted to twelve flats and was later reconverted to eight flats. The row was demolished c. 1962 for road widening. Belvedere Mews now occupies the site of the sheds behind.

CHALFORD WEST WITH HYDE.

A reverse view of the same sheds on the left, c. 1924. They were once a dyehouse belonging to David Farrar who had lived at adjacent Belvedere House. Note the shell of Iles Mill, burnt out in 1913.

Ballingers Lock and Roundhouse Pound, c. 1908, the time-honoured pastime of boys and grown men in progress in full view of Chalford Police Station, beyond them on the left.

The Companys Arms Inn and round house, c. 1920. Around 1800, the inn had regular coaches stopping here on their way to London, Bristol, and Gloucester. It is now a private house under the old name of Chalford Place, and is one of the oldest places in Chalford having links with the thirteenth-century de Chalkforde family.

An opposite view across Chalford (Ballingers, Belvedere) Mill Pond, c. 1920, the buildings on the main road to the left of the church were the forge and storehouse of Taysum, the blacksmith.

Chalford Mill and Belvedere House, c. 1930. Stroud Water Co. occupied part of the mill as a pumping station. Their successor, Severn Trent, is still there. Note the pine end of the house behind the tree (see opposite).

The steam engine, brought from the old Chalford Water Co's Valley Works (see page 40) in 1927, to power the pumps. Water was drawn from the Black Gutter, the former 100 springs of Chalford fame, and pumped up to the reservoirs on Minchinhampton Common.

A room in this house was used for many years, until demolition *c.* 1962, as a satellite surgery for the Eastcombe practice. Here, after surgery, Dr Hubert Crouch is looking along the road to Taysum's Forge.

In the early 1950s the Diocesan Architect decided the spire of Christ Church should be checked, and employed the Fire Brigade to use their extending ladder. Local Builder Ralph Everett is aloft.

The interior of Christ Church decorated for Harvest c. 1910. The east window is dedicated to the Ballinger family. The chancel screen was renewed and carved by Ernest Smith, a Gimson craftsman and foreman for Peter Waals.

The interest of this photograph taken in 1907 lies in the building beyond the Churchyard. On the left is Taysum's Forge; to its right, the upper floor of that building was used as a meeting room, the Chalford W.I. meeting there from its formation in the 1920s. Note the family in the Roundhouse doorway.

For the 1953 Coronation celebrations, Christ Church and School were flood-lit. Here is the effect at the school.

Those responsible for the lighting. Left to right: Bill Young, Bill Kirby, Alf Williams, -?-, -?-.

Chapel Bridge, c. 1955. Built over the canal to take the old Calfway from Bisley to Minchinhampton.

Demise of the bridge, c. 1962. The canal here was being culverted to re-align and widen the A419. The keystone was knocked out for the bridge to collapse over the culvert.

Aftermath of a fire at Bliss Mills, 1888, which destroyed the old mill by the main gate. It was noticed that the Stroud Volunteer Brigade Chief had difficulty in walking during the fire. It transpired that, in the haste of being called from his bed, he had put his trousers on back to front!

The new row of buildings and clock tower which replaced the ruins.

Above: When William Dangerfield died in 1894, the Bliss Mills site was leased to Arthur Harrison. In 1912, Sir Alfred Apperley bought the Mills from the mortgagees, Lloyds Bank. Here the Bank representative hands over the keys. Left to right: 'Captain' Barrett-Gilmore, Chief Mill engine driver; Thomas Burford, Chief Engineer; Willam Rowles & Dan Rowles, office staff. Bank representatives Sir Alfred Apperley and Charles Apperley.

Right: The site's yard always contained stacks of drying timber. A tramway was laid through the site to ease transport of the wood to the workshops. That site is now Chalford Industrial Estate.

The present-day bicycle centre Noah's Ark as a General Stores, c. 1930. It was such a store for three-quarters of this century before becoming a baby equipment store and then the bicycle centre.

The interior of the above store c. 1930. Miss Elsie Crook serving Miss Gwen Workman, who was later to work in the shop. The dog is only an advertising poster.

The main road, complete with horse bus, c. 1900. Left of the canal is Bliss Mills yard. The white-walled lay-by was for the County Council to store road material brought there by barge.

An enlargement of the upper right quadrant of the previous picture to show the little Seville's Upper Mill, the adjacent house being, now, The Hollies.

Central Garage, c. 1930, now Chalford Garage. Left to right: Leslie Hosier (later to be the H of H & L, Cainscross), Frank Hayward (later to own a garage at Chippenham), Lionel Padin (later to own Central Garage). Russian Oil Products petrol cost 1/- (5p) per gallon.

Bell Bridge at the bottom of Cowcombe Hill before the first straightening reconstruction of 1933.

Hallidays or Smarts Mill, *c.* 1925 adjacent to Bell Lock and Bridge when Peter Waals and his craftsmen were there carrying on the traditions of the Gimson/Barnsley School of Daneway. This property is now occupied by Arnold's Designs.

An interior of a workshop. In the foreground Percy Birchett, an original Gimson craftsman, at work.

Bell Lock and Red Lion Pound, c. 1908. On the left is the little bridge over the River Frome which took a footpath to the Bell Inn and the High Street. The three-storey house, by the Red Lion Inn, was one of Chalford's earliest red-brick houses.

Only a part of the up-platform of Chalford Station, beyond the field gate, shows in this early 1930s photograph, while, centre left, a goods wagon stands in the railway wharf sidings. These are now the Valley Trading site.

Chalford Station and wharf, c. 1910. The cattle pens, erected a few years earlier, saw great service for many years by Albert Crew of Wesley Farm, who periodically brought in trucks of cattle from Southern Ireland.

A slightly earlier Colville print of the same era, this time with a Railmotor trailer in the station siding. Who wanted to point out where they lived on Chalford Hill?

Chalford Station as opened on 2 August 1897. Here, passengers await the first train to London. The group on the right are the choir of Chalford Tabernacle who were going to sing at the Crystal Palace.

The same choir posed outside Chalford Tabernacle in 1899 for a photograph to be given to their retiring choirmaster, W.W. Taysum. They are, back row: (left to right) T. Trotman, J. Browning, Wm. Taysum, W.W. Taysum (choirmaster), F.C. Smart, Rev. D.R. Morgan (organ blower, behind), D. Wiltshire, F. Crook. Middle row: Julia Smith (organist), Mrs R. Webb, Miss Browning, -?-, Mrs Wm. Taysum, Mrs J.D. Jinton, Mrs W. Rowles, Mrs C. Pearce. Front row: Sarah Smith, -?-, Mrs D. Wiltshire, Kate Smart.

Only half of the crowd joining the trip. The rest of the up-platform was as crowded as this.
This August Bank Holiday trip was started by Harry Smart to take children away from the
debauchery of the notorious Chalford Feast.

Wesleyan Chapel and Lower High Street, c. 1905-8, being a view taken from above Bell Lock.
On the left in the foreground is Chalford Post Office, to its right is Fred Smart's General Stores,
complete with painted adverts.

Left: Fred Smart and son Jack, about the same period. Jack later kept the shop at Baughans Corner (see page 37).

Below: Jesse Miller and his dog, mid-1930s, on a Rack Hill path. Behind is the entrance to Rock House. It was said that the dog was Jesse's official taster.

Opposite above: Jesse (right) and his father in their shelter in Old Hills Wood, *c*. 1930. Jesse, who was an expert tree feller with axe and cross cut saw, lived, in later life, in a caravan along the track between Hyde Hill and Gypsy Lane.

Opposite below: West Rack Hill, 1874, part of a panoramic view of Chalford showing the terraces for the cloth racks of Hallidays Mill. Chalford Hill is on the skyline. The cottage centre right was to be enlarged, a few years later, to become Rock House.

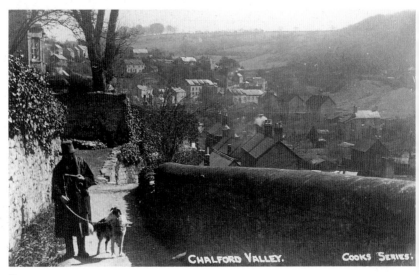

CHALFORD VALLEY.   COOKS SERIES.

Now, c. 1890, Rock House has been built, a little of the old cottage being visible behind it. Below, to its right, is the Bakery which, in 1953, became the Seventh Day Adventist Chapel. Arnold, the butcher, had the single-storey building (centre) as his shop.

Mid Rack Hill Section, 1874. The newly erected British School, now Chalford Hill Primary School, can be seen (centre skyline). The Limes and Stoney Riding now occupy part of the bare field in front. To the left of that field is Pooles Ground (see page 49).

The 'bread donkey' has always been a favourite character for photographers. Here, in the mid-1930s, Jenny waits patiently with her minder, Jimmy Rowles, in the High Street outside Saratoga Cottage.

An intrepid band of hikers on the canal path above Clowes Lock, around the time of the First World War. Do they know they have another three miles to go before reaching their goal?

The same view some twenty years later, about the time the canal was abandoned above Chalford.

Chalford

East Chalford from Cowcombe Hill, *c.* 1910-15. Sevilles Mill and pond are in the centre foreground. The boys (see page 55) were where the canal curves to enter the 'Narrows' between the Mill pond and railway viaduct. Note the Railmotor Engine Shed in the trees. It burnt down on 16 January 1916 and was never replaced.

An event for Millponds which occurred at least once a year: 'Mudding', clearing sediment to restore the holding capacity of the pond – send it on down to the next mill! Pictured in the mid-1930s, resting from their labours are: (left to right) Evan Young, Billy Phelps, Jack King, Charlie Liddiatt, Cyril Liddiatt, Harold Peacey and Fred Dean.

Baughan's delivery van outside his shop, Woodville Stores, at the junction of Coppice Hill and the High Street, c. 1912. J.H. Baughan is at the rear, and his son-in-law Ashley Young is with the horse. Previously, the Store had been a branch of Fawkes' store, Stroud.

Tanners Pitch to Valley Corner, c. 1923. There is evidence that The Mount, on the left, had been a posting house for coach horses, suggesting that an old road to Cirencester had run through the High Street before the present A419 was cut in 1815.

A reverse view from the Valley Inn, c. 1922. The square house is Green Court, the clothiers' house connected for centuries with Sevilles Mill. Above it at right angles is the roof of The Mount. At lower right note a little cottage squeezed between two taller cottages.

Right: A rather damaged photograph of that cottage in the early 1930s. On the left is Mrs Gleed with her daughters, Rose and Maisie, and grandson Omar. Mrs Gleed moved to the High Street after the war, the cottage being demolished in the mid-1960s.

Below: Valley Bridge, c. 1915-20. To the left is Tylers Mill, which was completely demolished by the mid-1930s. To the right is the Valley Inn, once the Clothiers Arms and before that a clothiers' house. Just to the left, before the lock chamber, there was little wharf.

The real start of the Golden Valley, *c.* 1890. The square white patch are the settling tanks for the Chalford Water Co., the pumping station being immediately behind on a level with Marley Bridge. Ashmeads Meadow is the field to the left of the white patch.

Ashmeads Mill, *c.* 1890, a woollen and later a silk mill, closed about 1897 and demolished piecemeal .The little cottage to its left was later the home of George and Dorcas Juggins (see pp. 2, 113-5).

The road from Valley Corner to Bakers Mill, c. 1930, a route for a half-hour Red Bus feeder service from Chalford Bus Terminus at the Grove to Bakers Mill, in the 1920s and 1930s, for Oakridge and Frampton Mansell. Truly one could get a bus through here!

Mr Charlie Mills bought the remains of Ashmeads Mill and its land to raise his family. The office part of the old mill had been made into a small cottage. In this photograph, on the footbridge which spanned the mill-race to connect the cottage with the canal towpath, Mrs Mills stands with her sons, George and Arthur (holding Spot), c. 1910.

Left: A damsel (not in distress!) on the path from Gassons through Drivers Wood, in the 1920s.

Below: The east section of the panoramic view dating from 1874 showing the terraces for the cloth racks of Sevilles Mill. That enclosure of part of Nash End Common had been awarded to Nathaniel Jones of Sevilles Mill. His executors sold it to Restall, a builder.

Coppice Hill and East Chalford, *c.* 1920. Compare this with the previous photograph to see how Restall developed the rack site.

Patiently waiting, *c.* 1912, outside the bakery in Coppice Hill, but not the one usually associated with 'Jenny the Donkey' – but then donkeys were common beasts of burden. The post box in the wall is still there!

Frank Colville's Cadover studio, c. 1905, at Stevensbridge, Coppice Hill, opposite the Tabernacle Sunday School rooms. Previously run by Mrs C.A. Dover, it was often called Spion Kop Studio. Frank came from a business in Guildford and Reading in about 1900 and moved to Swindon, to expand during the First World War.

This is said to be Frank Colville and his wife, and NOT a customer, in the 1920s. The location is not known.

Above: Mr William Blizzard, the noted herbalist, moved to the house, adding an adjoining annex to the studio for his shop and business. Here, in 1930, are some of his hives in the garden. More were kept in his orchard at the junction of Marley Lane with Cowcombe Hill. He and the local Medics worked closely together.

Right: Mr Blizzard and his two oldest sons, 1932. On the left is Ron, who followed his father in the business; on the right is Len, who became a noted cellist.

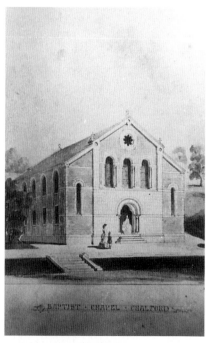

Left: The design of Chalford Tabernacle by the architect Tait of Leicester, to seat 450 adults. The Memorial Stone was laid by Mrs Eleanor Dangerfield on April 23 1873, the building being officially opened on 24 April 1874. The flat area and steps to the lower burial ground were never added.

Below: Interior of the Tabernacle, *c.* 1905. Frank Colville only had to take his kit across the road to take this photograph. The organ came from Highworth Church, near Swindon, and replaced the harmonium in the old Copse Chapel for two years before being moved to this purpose-built site.

Two

The Lynches

Marle Hill to Chalford Hill, *c.* 1940s. The Primary School is on the upper right, Commercial Road on the upper left. The pyramid-roofed building is France Congregational Church.

Gilder's View, 1962, showing the maze of paths and minor roads of Chalford Hill. The upper quarter shows Frith Wood surrounded by fields, now almost covered by the Manor and other developments.

The view north-west from the spring in Pooles Ground towards Commercial Road in the 1920s. Then, Pooles Ground was owned by the County Council, who intended to use the site for a new Primary School. The Post Office is behind the tree on the right.

Chalford Hill General Stores, 1890, situated at the Manchester and Birmingham House. The proprietor was Stafford. 'You want it, I have it!' Some forty years later it was the home and surgery of Dr Alfred Dill and, after the Second World War, Dr Ian Middleton (see page 120) after whom the adjoining road was named.

France Congregational Church, c. 1860-70. The land in the foreground was awarded to the church by the Nash End Common enclosure of 1869. When the church joined with the Baptist Church to build the British School in 1874, this piece was walled, partly with cut stone from the Old Vestry, and used by the School for recreational purposes.

Centenary celebration of the third church, July 1919. The building replaced the Old Vestry in 1819. The minister, H.W. Gurd, is seen in a frock coat in the centre of the group. He served for some thirty-five years until retirement. The church closed in 1985 and was sold for conversion into flats.

Work commenced in 1987. In February 1988, a large iron cistern was uncovered at the rear. It was recognised by two local engineers, John Bond and John Denley, as being a mid-Victorian boiler. Stroud and Dean Heritage Museums were alerted. Dean wanted it, but Stroud had first call. Through the efforts of Ian Mackintosh, it was acquired for Stroud. He arranged its removal to Kimmins Mill for safe-keeping.

The three 'saviours' watch the straps being fitted to lift it into Young's lorry on 4 November 1988. Left to right: Ian Mackintosh, John Denley, John Bond.

France Congregational Sunday School parade, c. 1912, on its way around the Primary School plot (see page 50) to the home of its Superintendent.

The parade assembled on the bank outside Clinton, the home of its superintendent, Joe Griffin. Chalford Band has led the parade.

A scene in the school plot, c. 1927. The plot (see page 50) had been turned into gardens by 1912 by headmaster Frank Webster. The older boys were encouraged to cultivate garden plots and sell the produce and also to enter the local Stroud Schools Competition, in which they were winners in 1927.

Chalford Hill School, Group 3, 1936. Back row: (left to right) Max Minchin, Eric Smart, Roy Griffin, Doug Cook, John Davis, Jim Wichard, Dennis Fawkes (?), Donald Lusty, Vic Townsend, Keith Shaylor. Third row: Iris Weaver, Eileen Stephens, Pauline Smith, Pam Skinner, Georgina Pegler, Mary Dean, Dulcie Brimfield, Margaret Ingram, Dorothy -?-, Noreen Munday. Teacher: Ethyl Arbon. Second row: Margaret Ollerenshaw, Yvonne David, Hazel Mills, Daphne Smith, Eileen Gardiner, Gwyneth Jefferies, Gwen David, June Dutton, Enid Webb, Brenda Creed. Front row: Frank Burford, Frank Jingle, David Castle, Les Kirby, John Samson, John Bingham, Mervyn Williams.

Left: Baker Gardiner with his delivery cart in Queens Square, outside the Duke of York Inn, early 1930s.

Below: South-west from behind and above the Duke of York, *c.* 1920. The outline of some buildings suggests some touching up. The large building, beyond the pitch, was the Fleece Inn.

The old Chalford Hill post office, c. 1920. Postmaster Austen Holmes and his family are in the garden. The post office was in a room of the house reached by a separate gate and door. It was later transferred to a separate building to the left, where it is today.

Commercial Road Store, c. 1930, which was owned by Harold Gardiner who had inherited it from an uncle. His assistant, Ashley Aldridge, stands in the doorway. The shop is now part of Clematis Cottage.

Wheatsheaf Cottage, Silver Street, in the 1930s. The interest lies in the building behind which was the Wheatsheaf Inn, closed in the 1950s. It was demolished, with others, by Stroud RDC to build the small Wheatsheaf Estate.

Lower Middle Hill, c. 1920, a view by Major, the Bisley photographer. The wall on the left then surrounded a triangle of garden ground, the cottage behind it being Chalford Hill Police Station.

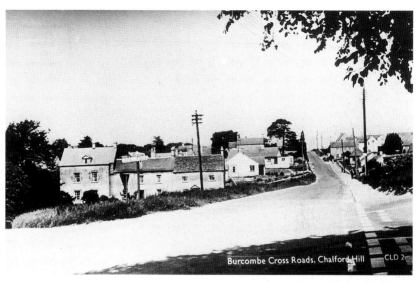

The same view some forty years later, the garden ground is now a parish green.

Middle Hill Farm, c. 1925, a busy threshing scene. It is believed that Farmer Mills is tending the portable engine.

Above: Primitive Methodist Chapel, *c.* 1905. Built 1823/4, it was one of the early chapels of the sect in the Stroud area. The building was gradually expanded over 150 years to the present-day Methodist Church. The Wesleyan Church, in the valley, had closed in 1957.

Left: Why was it a Charfield photographer who took this picture, *c.* 1900-1905? Standing: Jim Mayo, Tom Blackhouse (from Eastcombe). Seated: Harry Davis, Charlie Aldridge (last landlord of the Wheatsheaf). Jim Mayo was severely shell-shocked in the First World War and became general factotum for Dr Dill.

Gilder's View, 1962. The field, upper left quadrant, is now the Sports and Social Club site. Before, it had been forty lug allotments owned by the Bisley Feoffees.

South west from Hill Farm Orchard, 1937. Upper left, the church is partly obscured by trees. The recreation ground is beyond the trees on the skyline, while the parish bank is in front.

West from Upper Butlers Hill, *c.* 1930, looking towards the old post office. Just beyond the house on the right a pine end of the Court House Inn is visible. Note the open 'dicky' on the car.

Court House Inn, *c.* 1930. The name probably originated from its proximity to the Bisley Sub-Manor of Sturmyes Court, if it served as the venue of a Manorial Court. It was not a place where executions could take place, the nearest being at Sheepscombe. Mrs Butler was the landlady in 1930. It closed in 1956, the last landlord being Ron Clissold.

Southwest from Butlers Hill, c. 1930. The Church and Old Vicarage are on the left and the tall building on the skyline is France Lynch School, closed in 1932. Cottages to the right of the Vicarage were demolished about 1960.

Avenis, 1937. The post office, on the left, is now closed. Earlier, Mr Young had his bakery there, the hoist for lifting sacks of flour to the upper floor, being visible on the pine end. The first Red Bus service to Stroud started from the space in front of the Post Office.

Northwest from Woodlease over the Glen, to the Laregan, on the skyline, 1938. That house was a small private hotel in about 1900. Liddiatt's orchard, now the site of Council bungalows, is visible to the left of the post office.

St John the Baptist Church, seen here in 1907, was built in 1857. It was the first total church built to the design of the architect Bodley. It was the last of the four local churches to be built by the efforts of Thomas Keble, vicar of Bisley, and Edward Pyddoke was its first Priest in Charge.

A Colville photograph, c. 1907, of the interior of the church. Note his hat-rest!

Dedication of the churchyard cross, 1909, by the Rt Rev. Christopher Smythe, Bishop of Lebombo, standing in for the Bishop of Gloucester, who was ill. He was home on leave staying with his parents at Firwood, Brownshill. The verger is Mr Young.

North from the Parish Bank, c. 1937-8, where Mr Thrupp is tending his garden. Dorothea, now Dundry Lodge on the right, had been the home of Major General Pilchard, once Surgeon-General to King George V. At this time Mr Visger, 'doler-out' of gas masks, lived there.

At the north end of the village is the 'oasis' of the Kings Head. Even this view of 1970 has altered with minor developments.

Three

Oakridge Lynch
to Tunley

Jabez Whiting's cottage, c. 1910-15. A family album photograph. Jabez was a staunch Wesleyan and, on Sunday mornings between 6 and 7, would ride round the village on his bike, singing to rouse people to go to the prayer meeting. Note the grindstone, probably for grinding scythes.

Left: Coming up Drivers Wood, *c.* 1920, a common chore for country people, collecting wood to keep the home fires burning. Wesley railway bridge is visible (very faintly) on the upper left.

Below: South west down the valley from Farm Lane, *c.* 1903. In the centre is the partly-demolished Ashmeads Mill (p.40). A glimpse of shaded water above Boultings Lock to the left of the old 'haunted' cottage.

Frampton Farm, c. 1920. The bank below Wesley Bridge was denuded of trees in the First World War. Another view of the 'haunted' cottage in the field.

Frampton Farm, c. 1920. Farmer Hughes with some of his stock. He was drowned in Bakers Mill reservoir, about 1939.

Left: Drinking from the spout of the Holy Well trough in Farm Lane in summer, probably pre-1914. The boy on the bank could be the one on page 65.

Below: Church of St Bartholemew, c. 1910-12. The first of Keble's four churches. A south-west window was installed in memory of Mary Maude Plunket Birtwhistle, who died in 1913.

Church interior, c. 1910-12. Unfortunately, the chancel in this picture is too dark to enable us to distinguish the Ten Commandments which were painted on either side of the east window.

Oakridge School in winter, 1912. The trees had been planted on the green to commemorate the Coronation of King George V in 1911.

Oakridge School Group 1, 1923. Back row: (left to right) Eunice Robinson, Edith Gardiner, Nancy Hunt, ? Harris, Leslie Hunt. Second row: Phyllis Osborne, Marjorie Smith, Kathleen Smith, Nancy Buckell, Amy Duke, ? Harris, teacher Miss Williams. First row, standing: Raymond Kimber, Timmy Hunt, James Hussell, Stanley Woolls, James Young, John Hunt. Front row: Harry Hunt, Evelyn Selby, Alec Woolls, Doreen Young, Joyce Hunt, Maude Fowles, Kathleen Hewer.

Pencil drawing of Lower Wear Farm, c. 1914, drawn by a Belgian who was staying in the village.

The road from the Village Green joins Farm Lane and Butts Hill in this view postmarked 20 December 1908. The house on the left was the Post Office kept for many years by Mrs Wright and her daughter Ivy. The Wesleyan Methodist Church is faintly visible on the skyline.

Down Butts Hill, c. 1912. The grass area on the left was to be the site of the Dearmer Memorial. Earlier, a part of it had been fenced off as garden ground.

Above: The Dearmer Memorial, c. 1930-35, often called 'the Fountain'. Erected 'In memory of Mabel Dearmer who went from Oakridge, the place she loved best, to give help in Serbia, where she died of a fever at Kragujevatz on July 11th, 1915, aged 43, and of Christopher Dearmer, who died of wounds at Sulva Bay, in Gallipoli, on October 6th. 1915, aged 21,' Does history repeat itself?

Left: Believed to be Westley Cottage, now vastly altered, which is above the Memorial site on Butts Hill. Estimated to be c. 1912.

A summer scene over the Broadway to Frampton Mansell, from a vantage point on the upper road to Hillcroft. Penn farmhouse is on the middle right. Estimated to be about 1912.

Hillcroft, c. 1910-12, the home, shop and bakery of John Peacey, standing on the left.

John Peacey with his daughters outside the shop, about the same period. The boy and girl could be those on page 68 and are thought to be the children of Mr Lewis (see page 79), the photographer who probably took this picture.

John Peacey riding his motor cycle, probably in the 1920s. He learned to ride this Martynside when in his 70s; he was charged with speeding in his 80s, and met with an accident when he was 83 which resulted in a broken leg. He fretted to get well enough to ride again. Two of his daughters are with him.

Right: Cave Cottage, *c.* 1910 at the bottom of Sammels Hill behind Cobdens. Though much extended and altered it is still discernible. I wonder what village gossip was being exchanged?

Below: Above Sammels Hill in Chapel Lane, *c.* 1910-12, stood Mary Ann Gardiner's cottage where she kept a little shop. Again, though extended, its outline is still discernible. Note the tall tree for future reference.

Above: Mrs Rachel and Mary Ann Gardiner in the parlour at that time. Both had helped at the Dame School, held at the Wesleyan chapel (see page 123).

Left: A little further along Chapel Lane towards the chapel, visible in the distance. On the left is that tall tree (see page 76).

Right: The reverse view towards Mary Ann's cottage.

Below: The view from Chapel Lane over the Broadway towards The Taut and Frampton Mansell. It is probable that this photograph, and the previous five photographs, from a family album, were taken at the same time.

Methodist Chapel and schoolroom, 1947. The first Chapel, built about 1798, was replaced by this one in 1874. A Mr Pickersgill has been named as the founder of the church.

A group gathered outside the Chapel, postmarked 2 September 1907. The occasion is not known. Fourth from the left in the back row is Frank Gardiner of Tunley and the bearded man on the right is believed to be Seth Peacey.

A Whitsuntide treat was an annual event for Sunday Schools. Usually this meant a parade round the village. If you had no band to lead the singing, a regular feature, then you had to take your portable harmonium. Here, in the 1920s, Mr Lewis is ready to play while John Peacey is probably selecting the hymn.

After the tea came the games and sports in the playing field. Here, about 1910, the contestants are waiting for the signal for the 'off', from the minister.

Above: They're away!

Left: A cottage in Becca's Hill, *c.* 1912, opposite the Spring. A very faded caption suggests it was Caleb's Cottage. It has seen several renovations and alterations to its present form.

A view from a vantage point above Becca's Hill in the 1920s. On the centre skyline, a pine end of the Butchers Arms, with logo, is visible.

The landlord, Frank Gardiner, of the Butchers Arms in his garden. Estimated mid-1930s.

Southwest from Becca's Hill, late 1930s, looking across the Broadway to Penn House, Westley Farm and Aston Down in the distance.

This cottage has been identified as the present 'Broadway', the roof lines either side having been raised to the centre level. Estimated to be *c.* 1910. Is grocery or bread being delivered?

Right: The dilapidated house on the right, adjacent to the path from the Broadway to the upper road, was captioned 'Jane Young's old home'. The late Dr Allen, who lived in Oakridge as a boy, related that the house fell into decay because no one would live there after a ghost was seen on the stairs. It was replaced with a bungalow many years ago.

Below: School headmaster, Mr Allen, with his elder daughter, Violet, riding bareback in the Broadway near the path to Jane Young's old home. Estimated to be in the first eight years of the twentieth century.

The track from Daneway over Whitehall canal bridge past Trillies hamlet to Iles Green (left) and Far Oakridge (right) on the skyline.

Cottage at Trillies, c. 1920. Essential repairs to the thatch are being carried out.

The view from Peyton's Grove, below Hillhouse Wood, Tunley, to Oakridge Farm, at Far Oakridge. Estimated to be about 1910-14.

The Holy Brook runs through Tunley parallel to the Daneway Road before reaching Peyton's Grove. In this photograph dating from about 1905, the path from Tunley towards Far Oakridge crosses the stone bridge near a dilapidated byre.

Above: The junction of the road from Far Oakridge and Waterlane with Tunley Lane, left, and Hillhouse Lane, right, to Daneway, in the summertime of 1910. Note the thatched cottage.

Left: The same cottage in Hillhouse Lane from the junction.

Right: Serious conversation in that summer at the gate of the old cottage. Had she been up to Oakridge for stores?

Below: The second building along Hillhouse Lane from the junction c. 1912. The children in the garden are the sisters of Dr Allen, who also took the photograph.

The same building, c. 1905, was a pair of semi-detached cottages. Mrs Gardiner at the left doorway, Mrs Bucknell, with daughters Sophie and Annie, at the right doorway, Mrs Bucknell being wife of the blacksmith. Mrs Gardiner and Mrs Bucknell were sisters.

The cottages were converted in the 1950s to one dwelling by Dr Snow, a retired doctor from Saudi Arabia, who renamed it The Old Forge.

Four

The South Eastern Villages

The workshop of Ernest Gimson and Ernest and Sidney Barnsley at Pinbury Park, *c.* 1895. Note the plasterwork against the wall, the part-made chair, and the inlay on the coffer.

Mr Arthur Pearman, landlord of the Bricklayers Arms, and his wife, in a field of their smallholding at the Inn. The year would be about 1920.

Mr Pearman ready to take milk to Hill House. Mrs Pearman is in the doorway.

The man-trap which was stored in a room of the inn for many years. It had come into the possession of the landlord in settlement of an outstanding debt.

The inscription on the man-trap shows it was made for Thomas Hancox of Daneway House in 1794. It was made by a local blacksmith for the Hancox estate.

In the nineteent century this was a common sight in pubs, a copper boot filled with ale or scrumpy and pushed into the ashes of the fire to mull the brew.

This view, from the canal towpath across the summit lock to the Bricklayers Arms, was taken in May 1911 with the fruit trees in blossom. The garden and lock are now part of the Inn car park. Note the landau-type car on the road.

View across Daneway Wharf and Basin in May 1911 down the valley to Frampton Mansell.

Daneway Wharf and Gardiner's Sawmill from Hillhouse Lane. The appearance of the canal and wharf suggest a date of about 1896, when the canal was in a very derelict state, before restoration by the Councils' consortium.

The same view c. 1905. Compare with the previous photograph. There is activity on the wharf, and more outbuildings at the Sawmill.

Compare this photograph with the following two. In this view down the six-lock flight to Whitehall Bridge the canal is empty, but the lock-gates do not look too bad. The appearance suggests a date of about 1896 about the time of the de Salis report.

Now, there is some water in the Canal and Wharf Basin and a little repair seems to have been done but it seems to be falling into disuse again. Therefore, the date is probably 1912.

In this final photograph of the sequence from May 1917, the rot appears to have set in, and only ten years before abandonment! Even then, looking at this photograph, is it any wonder that the urge is there to restore the waterway?

Charles Smith of the Victoria Steam Joinery Works, Chalford, now Chalford Chairs, with his agent Billy Farmer, at Daneway, *c.* 1890. He had bought the Daneway Estate, for the timber it contained, but sold it in 1897 to Earl Bathurst.

The summit level of the canal, winding its way towards the lengthman's cottage and the Sapperton Tunnel mouth, faintly visible to the right, about 1912.

The intrepid band of hikers of page 35 have reached their goal, the Western Portal of Sapperton Canal Tunnel.

A last look down the Valley from below Sapperton Church, in February 1913. Mrs Whiting has the fire burning in the lengthman's cottage. The white building behind the tree is the Bricklayers Arms.

A Denis Moss photograph, c. 1910, looking along the lower road to the Sapperton Church of St Kenelm. The building on the right, undergoing repair, became the village stores.

An interior of St Kenelm's church, c. 1920. A portion of the small gallery is visible on the right. Note the carved ends to the pews.

Right: A close-up of two carvings. These are said to have been removed from the old Sapperton House, home of Sir Henry Poole and later Sir Robert Atkyns, before the house was burnt down *c.* 1735. They were then adapted for this use in the later church restoration of that period.

Below: View from the church to the main road, *c.* 1930. The marked cottage is Pear Tree Cottage. The building beyond is the police station on the other side of the road. Cultivation of the gardens suggests late spring.

SARPERTON 15

The main road and part of the school on the left. The presence of the motor cycle suggests the photograph dates from the 1920s. The pupils asppear to be engaged in physical education of some sort.

Sapperton School group, *c.* 1901-2. Note the hob-nailed soles of the boots of the boys in the front row.

Above: An opposite view along the road to the school, hidden by the tree. The tranquillity of the road and the dress suggest a date in the early 1930s.

Right: The Leasomes *c.* 1905, the house that Ernest Gimsom designed and built for himself on land given by Earl Bathurst, when he moved Gimson and the Barnsleys from Pinbury Park to Daneway House in 1902. Their improvements to Pinbury made him desirous of living there himself. Fire destroyed the roof of Leasomes in 1940 and it was reroofed with tiles.

Left: Ernest Gimson's gardener was Charlie Aldridge. Here, probably in the second decade of the century, are his wife and son standing ouside the door of their cottage.

Below: The Bell, *c.* 1910-1915, when Mrs Harrison was landlady. It is now a very popular 'oasis' for the district.

Manor Farm, *c.* 1920s, the largest farm in the Sapperton area, previously called Court Farm. At that time the Chamberlain family lived there. It appears that the Chamberlain who farmed there during the Second World War, was threatened with eviction by the Agricultural Board if he did not mechanise, so he had to buy his first tractor which he considered to be a poor beast compared to his horses.

Noah's Ark, *c.* 1932-3, one of the Cirencester Park Lodges. It looks to be a nice Spring or Autumn day. The little girl is Kathleen Whiting.

But now the winter has come. The same little girl by the village green.

St Luke's Church, *c.* 1920, built to a design of J. Parish in 1844. A few years ago it was saved from closure by a few dedicated villagers and is now in the multi-benefice of the Rector of Sapperton.

Above: Opening day, 1924. Congregating outside the Memorial Chapel in Pike Lane. The chapel was built on land bought by Charles Clark of The Downs from the Bathurst Estate. Cattle were apt to peer through the windows from the adjoining field during services.

Right: View up Pike Lane, 1924, the farthest building being the Baptist chapel, closed in 1994 and now a private house. For several years the top cottage was the Manse. The second, with porch, was the old Mission Room, replaced by the Chapel. The three cottages formed part of the endowment made to the Chapel by Clark.

Left: When two farmers, J. Ratcliffe of Beacon Tump Farm (left) and Charles Clark of The Downs Farm, conversed like this, then it must have been serious.

Below: The Downs, *c.* 1910, home of Charles E. Clark, JP, County Council Alderman, Deacon, and benefactor, for many years, of the Baptist chapels at Chalford and Frampton Mansell. Until the mid 1930s it was the venue of the Whitsun Treat of the Sunday Schools of the two chapels.

Garden party at The Downs, 20 July 1907, the first garden party arangd by Mr and Mrs Clark to raise funds for the renovation of Chalford Tabernacle and schoolroom. It became a regular event until the First World War, and was an annual job for Frank Colville too. Miss Florrie Clark is holding the donkey's reigns. Taysum, the Blacksmith, wears the conical hat.

Tea ladies from the Chapel's 1907 party.

The road to Sapperton, c. 1907. The Crown Inn is on the left. In the garden of the cottage above, a small village store was later built.

The Crown Inn, c. 1920. The name on the cart appears to be 'Lewis', but the crate with the rounded top is puzzling.

The Oak Inn at Pucks Mills, c. 1901. A round drying tower for Pucks Mill stood about where the tall chimney stands on the left. The mill had only been demolished a few years previously.

Enlarged view of the Oak, c. 1901-3. Note the beams of the lower gates of Pucks Mill Upper Lock. The landlord, Mr Peart, his wife, and daughter, Alice, stand in the yard. Pucks Mill Farm was run from the Oak.

Across the Manor Grounds to Wesley Bridge in the 1920s. The two houses are Little Hattons, and Hattons (partly hidden). The railway here climbs Sapperton Bank, beloved by train spotters for 150 years.

But now, with steam gone, a diesel coasts over the viaduct hauling an enthusiasts' special on 20 February 1977 in wintry conditions. The GWR must have paid the owners of Frampton Manor House well to block their view with the viaduct, although it was originally a wooden structure.

Bakers Mill Reservoir, c. 1920s. This truly was a reservoir, constructed by the Thames and Severn Canal Co. to collect water to serve the locks down to Chalford.

A much earlier opposing view over Bakers Mill Lock in the 1880s; to the right of the lock there was sufficient space for a small wharf for coal to be off-loaded for Oakridge and Frampton Mansell and Oakridge Mill.

Bakers Mill House and Old Mill c. mid-1930s, had been called Twissels Mill from a previous owner. Home of Bee the Otter and successors, it has also been used for a variety of TV drama productions.

Wesley Bridge, 5 June 1965. The 5.30pm Saturdays-only football train from Swindon to Gloucester, hauled by 2–6–2T BR Class 8 82039, the last working of this train by steam.

Five

Individuals, Groups and Occasions

Dorcas and George Juggins, 1960s, at the Butchers Arms, Oakridge, their 'spiritual' home at that time.

Dorcas photographed in the 1960s with, it is thought, the lodger, Ernie Dukes. The background seems to be a farm.

George with his mother-in-law in the 1920s. George and Dorcas took it in turns to push Mrs Townsend in the wheelchair to Stroud, the procedure being that one pushed while the other rode a bike, swapping over at intervals. The old Lloyds Bank branch in the High Street seems to be the one in the background. (See opposite page for the 'history' of George and Dorcas.)

Chalford Tabernacle senior branch of the International Order of Good Templars 1911, taken in the Tabernacle Schoolroom. Back Row: Lily Pidgeon, Dorcas Townsend (Mrs G. Juggins), Elsie Oborn (Mrs Robbins), Trevor Webster, William Gardiner, Florence Browning, George Swinford. Fourth row: Lily Oborn, Jessie Carrington (Mrs Boyce), Mabel Browning, Jane Gardiner, Harry Critchley, Gladys Kilminster (Mrs A. Davis), Ethel Oborn, Douglas Webster. Third row: Hilda (?) Oborn, Mrs Chas. Gardiner, Marjorie Smart, Charles A. Gardiner, Beatrice Smart, Albert H. Griffin, Robert H. Taysum, Lily Tyler (Mrs G. Miles), Percy G. Tyler, Charles Close. Second row: Celia Rowles (Mrs Harry Orchard), Mr Pidgeon, Renee Selwyn, Stanley Griffin, James Harry Smart, Charles Herbert, Sally Mills (Mrs Percy Rodway), Frederick G. Tyler, Daisy Gardiner (Mrs Beauchamp), Miss Griffin. Front row: Bert Dean, Daisy Phelps, Eva Poole (Mrs Messenger), Albert King, Charles Pidgeon, Eva Pearce (Mrs Bert Hunt), Ivy Mills.

George and Dorcas were part of the folklore of Chalford and the surrounding district. Dorcas was the daughter of Mr and Mrs Townsend who ran a horse bus service to Stroud and Cirencester, Mrs Townsend being the driving force of the business. It was said that she kept Dorcas in a wheelchair until she was twelve. George was born at Burleigh, it is not known how they met. They were married at Chalford Mission Chapel and when asked 'Wilt thou have this woman ... ', George replied: 'That's what I be come yer for'. They both worked at St Mary's Mill for the Chalford Stick Company for many years. George retired from there as Yard Foreman, he would tell you, although he was the only one in the yard gang. Dorcas was in demand for many years on local farms being considered the finest 'turnip-hoer' in the area. They never had any children. It was said that mother-in-law slept in the same bed as they did, a lodger taking her place when she died. The longest resident lodger was Ernie Dukes. This was the basis of much ribaldry, and George became the butt for the local girls, especially on the last bus from Stroud at night. The front seat upstairs was always kept for him if he had been seen in the queue. Dorcas was illiterate, so George would send an invitation to himself to go to a fictitious function in order to get a night out. They were both staunch Conservatives, decorating their bike with the Union Jack and blue ribbons to go to the polling station at election time. The polling clerk always had to clear the room so that he could ask Dorcas who she wished to vote for. Invariably her answer was: 'Gie I the Blue 'un'. Drink was their weakness, and they were both great snuff takers. Dorcas could also out-swear any seasoned trooper, having a masterly control of 'the full beauties of the English language'. In mid-life they acquired a donkey, which Dorcas used for her farm work. They also had a menagerie of fowls and animals which used their home, including a guinea pig which occupied half of the table. George died in about 1970 and poor Dorcas was burnt to death in a fire at the cottage in 1975.

Christ School class in the 1920s. In the centre of the front row is Jack Damsell.

Chalford had a thriving Horticultural Society at the beginning of the twentieth century. Colville took this photograph of the 1909 Show, which could have been at Firwood, Brownshill.

The forerunner of the Young Conservatives was the Primrose League, very active in Chalford in Edwardian times. It had a meeting room in Hallidays Mill, and seems to have held a fête each year. This is another Colville photograph.

Another annual event in Chalford was Ashmeads Fair, held in Ashmeads Meadow (see page 40). Colville captured this scene in 1913. The fête was not held during the First World War, but restarted in 1919.

Chalford Post Office staff, c. 1902. Back row: (left to right) John Hawkes, A. Price, J. Baxter, J. Jones, G. Workman, S. Barnett. Front row: Miss L. Gardiner, Miss Wear (postmistress), Miss K. Gardiner. In front: L. Griffin (telegraph boy).

Officers and NCOs, Chalford Section, Volunteer Training Corps, First World War – a Grand Dads' Army! Back row: (left to right) Fred Smart, Dan Wiltshire, ? Halliday, Frank Ridler Dutton, Harry Marmont. Seated: Fred Furley, Wilfred White, two officers of whom one was ? Clissold, Frank Webster, Augustus Hook.

Right: 'Three little maids from school are we', *c.* 1905: Daisy Gardiner, Marjorie Smart, Ethyl Phelps.

Below: Chalford Second XI, 1922/3. Back row: (left to right) Len Freeman, Ellis Gardiner, Gordon Harrison, Gilbert Ollerenshaw, Arthur Davis. Middle row: Harold Jefferies (captain), George Dean, D. Rowles (Vice-Captain). Front row: C. Browning, Gilbert Gardiner, Tommy Hunt, Charlie Lester, Billy Mayo.

Chalford over 50s Cricket Team, c. 1948-50. Back row: (left to right) Ernie Peacey, Bill Young, George Dean, Gilbert Ollerenshaw, Dr Ian Middleton. Front row: G. Workman, Charlie Halliday, Archie Ward, George Davis, Otto Griffin, Ellis Gardiner.

France Lynch church Sunday school treat, c. 1910-12, gathered on the parish bank. The day school is behind the banner on the right. If the date is correct, the vicar (fourth from the left on the third row) is David Wade-Evans.

An organised assembly in France Lynch playing field in 1911 for Colville to take his photograph. He has them assembled on the site of the old cricket square, with their backs to the Parish Bank.

They are not quite so formal in 1935 for King George V's Silver Jubilee, but are just a part of the carnival. The top hat is worn by Yvonne Fuller.

France Lynch School orchestra, *c.* 1922. Back row: (left to right) Rose Ford, Duncan Young, Ron Minchin, Keith Jackson, Bill Cambridge. Front row: Freda Minchin, Miss Cresswell (infant teacher), Mr Marmont (headmaster), Blanche Young (teacher), Joan Young.

Maypole dancers at Oakridge Church Fête, 1910. The Oakridge School headmaster, Mr Allen, is on the left; and the teacher, Miss Maud Williams, is at the rear.

Oakridge Dame School, c. 1890, was started at the Wesleyan Chapel by Elizabeth Whiting, who died in 1874. It was continued by Susannah Whiting with the help of Rachel Gardiner and, later, Mary Ann Gardiner. Closed by the Education Act of 1902, it was said to provide a better education than the National School. Back row: (left to right) Miss Susannah Whiting, Albert Gardiner, ? Twissel, ? Whiting (or Sidney Smith), ? Hunt, Mildred Whiting, Cornelius Gardiner, Amelia Gardiner, Alice Newcome, Maria Gardiner, William Gardiner. Middle row: Annie Peacey, Sarah Hunt, Christopher Gardiner, Elisha Dean, Ellen Gardiner, Edmund Rowles. Front row: -?-, Alice Gardiner, William Young, Helena Whiting, Ethyl Gardiner, Wilfred Gardiner.

A wheelbarrow race in the 1930s, at a Methodist Chapel Whitsun treat.

Oakridge Village Players, the cast of *The Village Wedding*, in the 1920s. Back row: (left to right) Sam Gardiner, Jim Gardiner, Miss E. Brinkworth, Miss Irene Restall, Mrs A. Ingram, Gilbert Hunt. Front row: Tom Gardiner, Kate Young, Fred P. Gardiner, Miss Louisa Gardiner, Walter Young.

Stroud Cricket League, 1907, the Oakridge team. Back row: (left to right) Jim Gardiner, -?-, F.P. Gardiner, -?-, Harry Gardiner (Seth), -?-, Wilfred Gardiner (Caleb). Front Row: -?-, Bernarl Gardiner, Tommy Gardiner, Henry Wright, -?-, Frank Gardiner.

Oakridge Football Club, 1954. Back row: (left to right) R. Dangerfield, Mr Short, Mr Hamp, L. Gardiner, L. Gommers, T. Hunt, G. Hunt. Middle row: S. Short, J. Herbert, R. Goodfield, P. Gardiner, J. Fry, G. West. Front row: A. Aldridge, ? Aldridge, G. Smith, R. Kimber, H. Hunt.

Haymaking at Frampton Mansell, 1930s: Bill Roberts, Sam Ash, and Arthur Roberts. A rope sledge was often used to haul haycocks to the rick on these steep banks.

Children of Sapperton School often put on plays for the village. These are scenes from their pre-1914 production of *Green Broom*.

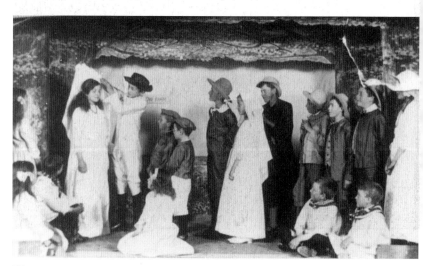

A family album photograph captioned 'Uncle Arthur', taken in Oakridge with Frampton Mansell in the background. What better photograph of a countryman could you get?

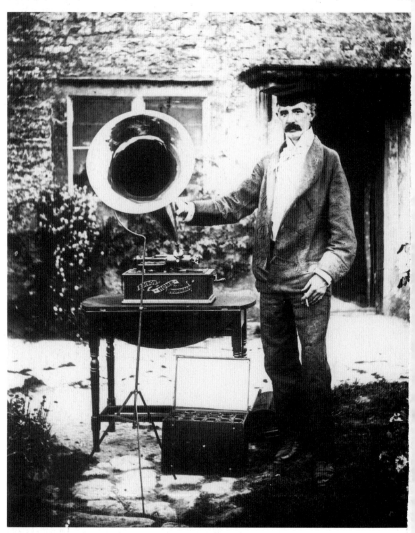

John Taylor in the 1920s. Known as Uncle Jack to many children in Chalford and Oakridge, John Taylor worked at the Mount Pleasant sorting office of the GPO in London and married Mary Gardiner of Tunley. They spent many holidays in Oakridge and France Lynch, and eventually retired to Chalford. He was keen on music hall and magic and had a wide variety of props. In this picture he is believed to be standing outside his sister-in-law's home in Oakridge. One record for his phonograph, I remember, was *The Laughing Policeman*.